THE SONGHAY EMPIRE

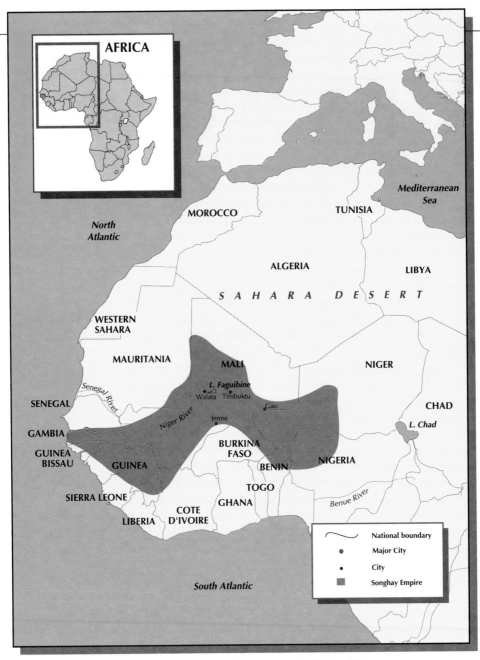

The powerful Songhay Empire extended across much of West Africa.

~African Civilizations~

THE SONGHAY EMPIRE

David Conrad, Ph.D.

A First Book

Franklin Watts
A Division of Grolier Publishing
New York / London / Hong Kong / Sydney
Danbury, Connecticut

Photographs copyright ©: Nik Wheeler/Corbis: pp. 7, 23, 24, 42; Adria La Violette: pp. 9, 56; Chris Rainier/Corbis: p. 10; Nicolas le Corre/Gamma Liaison: p. 12; Werner Forman Archive/Art Resource, NY: pp. 15, 28; David Conrad: pp. 17, 34; Charles & Josette Lenars/Corbis: p. 19; Trip/Trip/Viesti Associates, Inc.: pp. 33, 37; Robert Holmes/Corbis: p. 50; Trip/J Sweeney/Viesti Associates, Inc.: p. 54.

Library of Congress Cataloging-in-Publication Data

Conrad, David C.
   The Songhay empire / David Conrad. — 1st ed.
      p.   cm. — (A first book)   (African civilizations)
   Includes bibliographical references and index.
   Summary: A survey of the history and culture of the West African Songhai Empire that flourished from the 1460s until the 1590s, when it was conquered by Morocco.
   ISBN 0-531-20284-4
   1. Songhai Empire—History—Juvenile literature. I. Title. II. Series III. Series: African civilizations.
   DT532.27.C66   1998
   966.2'018—dc21   97-31288
                                                          CIP
                                                           AC

CONTENTS

INTRODUCTION

The Songhay Empire was the last of three great empires that existed in the Western Sudan. The Western Sudan is a vast geographical region south of the Sahara Desert and north of the forest belt of coastal West Africa.

At its peak, the Songhay Empire stretched from what is now western Mali to the Hausa kingdoms in what is now northern Nigeria. The empire developed along both sides of the Niger River, which flowed in a great curve through the entire country from west to east.

An empire is made up of many kingdoms, formed when one kingdom becomes more powerful than the others. The more powerful king creates an empire by conquering his weaker rivals and making their lands part of his.

Inhabitants of the great cities of the Songhay Empire, such as Jenne, included Muslim businessmen involved in trading goods across the Sahara Desert. The mosque was the focus of Muslim community life and Islamic learning. This mosque in Jenne, located beyond the market, was built in 1905.

In the case of Songhay, the original kingdom was Gao, a city on the Niger River. The Kingdom of Gao began to develop as early as A.D. 680. Its kings gradually increased their power until they began to rule over neighboring peoples. Together, all those peoples came to be known as Songhay.

By the 1460s the Kingdom of Gao had expanded to become the Songhay Empire. The empire lasted until the 1590s, when it was conquered by Morocco.

THE PEOPLE OF GAO

The Songhay Empire was composed of many different peoples who made their livelihoods from the Niger River and its bordering lands. The Sorko people were fishermen who built and operated boats and canoes. The Gow people relied on hunting such river animals as crocodiles and hippos. People known as the Do farmed the rich lands bordering the river.

The homeland of some Songhay ancestors was in Dendi. It was located along the Niger River between Niamey and Tillabery in what is now the Republic of Niger. Some legends say the Sorko came from the south in search of hippos. The local

The Songhay Empire included many different ethnic groups, members of which still live in the region today. The woman seen here with her grandson has tattooed lips, a sign that she is a descendant of a noble Songhay family.

people accepted the leadership of the warlike Sorko, who became recognized as the masters of the Niger River.

A different legend was recorded by *Muslim* writers who lived in Timbuktu, an important city near the Niger River. According to the story, the Songhay people worshiped a monster fish-god that wore a ring in its nose and was the spiritual guardian of the river. It is said that a stranger, who arrived in Gao from somewhere to the east, killed the creature. This could be a storyteller's way of

During the time of the Songhay Empire, trade goods were transported across the Sahara Desert on the backs of camels. A camel trainer in the Western Sudan poses with a camel.

describing how a chief of the Tuareg people of the Sahara Desert came from the east and conquered the leader of the Niger River boatmen.

The camel-riding Tuareg were among the earliest people of the region. They periodically rode out of the Sahara to establish camps near the Niger River. There they stored their trade goods and conducted business with others who used the river. Some of these Tuareg camps eventually grew into towns and cities.

In about A.D. 679 a Tuareg chief, Za Aliemen, made his capital at Kukiya, which was downriver from Gao and near the present-day frontier between Mali and Niger. Aliemen founded the first known Songhay dynasty, or line of rulers. They carried the title of *za*, which means king in the Tuareg language.

GAO BECOMES A KINGDOM

Between 750 and 950, the city of Gao became an increasingly important trade center for goods being transported across the Sahara Desert. These goods included gold, salt, slaves, kola nuts, leather, dates, and ivory.

Some of the ivory was from elephant tusks. However, *archaeologists*, scientists who study the way humans lived a long time ago, have recently learned that the Songhay also exported hippo tusks from Gao. Furniture makers in North Africa and Spain preferred hippo ivory because it retained its pure white color after it was cut into pieces. The pieces were then inlaid into beautifully carved wooden furniture.

The trade in such valuable products made the

Ancestors of contemporary Berbers played a key role in trans-Saharan trade.

Songhay rulers wealthy, because they taxed all of the goods moving in and out of their territory. This rich trade caused Gao to become their capital city, although Kukiya remained the place of the king's permanent residence.

Early West African traders did not use the kind of money that is in use today. One way they did business was through the barter system, in which one type of product was traded for another. Also, for many centuries they used small shells called cowries as currency. These shells were inconvenient, however, because their value was so small. It took many of them to buy anything. When the German traveler Heinrich Barth visited Timbuktu in 1853–54, he paid 13,500 shells for a single piece of cloth.

Many of the merchants involved in the trans-Saharan trade were Berber people. They were Muslims who traded with the people on the southern edge of the Sahara, including the Songhay. In Gao a commercial and residential area with *mosques* was established for the Muslim merchants. Later, as *Islam* became increasingly influential, the *za* of Gao allowed a mosque to be built in his own part of the city.

Songhay oral history—historical reports that are passed on from generation to generation by word of mouth—states that in the year 1010 Za Kossoi officially converted to Islam. This improved his relations with the Muslim traders. It also gave him spiritual authority over his Muslim subjects and so increased his power.

Knowledge of Songhay history was greatly increased in the 1950s, when archaeologists made an important discovery in the village of Saney, near

Gao. They found tombstones made of Spanish marble with Arabic inscriptions. These tombstones marked the graves of the kings of Gao, including Abu Abdallah Muhammad, who died in the year 1100. In Arabic, the name Abdallah means slave of Allah (God), signifying someone who is a devout Muslim. This suggests that by then the kings of Gao were firmly attached to the Islamic faith, and their trade network extended all the way to Spain. Apparently they were wealthy enough to import such expensive goods as marble.

THE SUNNI DYNASTY

Early in the 1300s the *za* dynasty of Gao was replaced by a new line of rulers. The new rulers carried the title of *sunni* or *shi,* the meaning of which is uncertain.

At this time, the Mali Empire, which lay upriver from Songhay country, was the dominant force in the region of the upper Niger River. For hundreds of years the wealth and importance of Gao had been increasing steadily because of its trade across the Sahara. Attracted by Gao's prosperity, the emperor of Mali, Mansa Musa, conquered the

The Jingerebir mosque at Timbuktu is thought to have been founded in 1325 by Mansa Musa, the emperor of Mali.

Kingdom of Gao in the early 1300s. Mali then controlled the Songhay people's trade routes and collected taxes from their rulers.

The second *sunni* of Gao, Sulayman Mar, later led the Songhay army against Mali. In this way he regained Gao's independence from Mali in about 1375.

SUNNI ALI, THE SORCERER KING

The greatest hero of Songhay legend is Sunni Ali Ber of the *sunni* dynasty. In the oral traditions recounted by Songhay storytellers, he is remembered as a courageous ruler who built the Songhay Empire and a *sorcerer* who had magical power. He is still known as the "sorcerer king."

Ali's mother was from the town of Fara, whose people were not strict Muslims. Their religious leaders were *diviners* and sorcerers who practiced the religion of their ancestors, worshiping spirits and showing respect for ancestors. They were among the best educated people in their society. They communicated with the spirit world to determine the causes

A diviner receives messages from spirits by casting cowrie shells, much as dice are thrown, and then interpreting the fall of the cowries. The diviner also consults the Koran. Strict Muslims object to such mixing of religious traditions, which was—and still is—a common practice in the Western Sudan.

of problems that arose in their community. Once the spirits had helped them identify the problems, traditional priests performed sacrifices in honor of the spirits. In this manner, priests were able to solve problems and cure diseases with the help of the spirits.

This was the community in which Ali grew up, watched over by his mother and uncles. He was a Songhay prince and received some basic instruction in Islam. But when he reached manhood, he displayed more faith in the ancient ways of magic and sorcery. Later, when he came to the throne, he ruled over the Muslim traders and scholars who lived in the cities. Most of his subjects, however, were non-Muslim farmers, hunters, and fishermen of the countryside. Sunni Ali governed effectively by maintaining his association with both Islam and the religion of his ancestors.

Ali became *sunni* of Gao and the lands surrounding the city in about 1464. An ambitious ruler and military leader, Sunni Ali began his expansion of Gao by attacking the neighboring peoples who often raided areas that the Songhay regarded as their territory. Among those he attacked were the Mossi, the Fulani, and the Dogon.

Once Sunni Ali had cleared Gao of its most immediate dangers, he turned his attention and his army to conquering Timbuktu, the second most important city in the region.

TIMBUKTU

Timbuktu was founded in about 1100 by the Tuareg people. Populated mainly by Muslims, it

The Dogon village of Irel is situated along the base of the Bandiagara cliffs, not far from the Niger River.

had three large mosques and several smaller ones. By the 1400s Timbuktu had become an important gathering place for Muslim scholars of religion and other subjects from all over North Africa and the Middle East.

The Muslim scholars of Timbuktu studied and wrote in the *Arabic* language. They viewed themselves and their city as unique. They also believed that their authority came not from rulers such as Sunni Ali but from Allah. They defied Sunni Ali and refused to acknowledge his authority over them. As a result, Sunni Ali considered them enemies.

At this time Muhammad-n-Adda was governor of Timbuktu. He feared the growing power and approaching army of Sunni Ali. The governor had been friendly with the powerful Muslim scholars and Tuareg leaders of Timbuktu, who were Sunni Ali's enemies. Hoping to escape punishment, Muhammad-n-Adda sent a letter to Sunni Ali saying that he would be glad for Timbuktu to be ruled by the Songhay Empire. Governor Muhammad-n-Adda died, however, before Sunni Ali and his troops ever reached Timbuktu.

Muhammad-n-Adda's son, Umar, became the next governor. Umar was not afraid of Sunni Ali as his father had been. Umar and the other leading men of Timbuktu did not believe that they should be under the authority of the Songhay kings. So Umar sent Sunni Ali an insulting message, bragging that he could fight off any attack by the Songhay armies.

In about 1469 Sunni Ali and his Songhay army arrived across the river from Timbuktu. The people of Timbuktu feared that Sunni Ali would inflict a terrible punishment upon them for defying his authority and cooperating with his enemies, the Tuareg. The Tuareg king supplied the frightened citizens with a caravan of 1,000 camels, on which many fled to Walata, a city in the Sahara Desert.

Meanwhile, Umar regretted the insulting letter he had sent Sunni Ali. In an attempt to make peace, he ordered boats to help Sunni Ali and the Songhay army cross the Niger River. Before the army entered Timbuktu, Umar escaped to Walata, leaving his brother al-Mukhtar to face the dreaded Songhay army.

When Sunni Ali crossed the river and arrived in Timbuktu he named al-Mukhtar the new governor. He allowed his troops to burn part of the city and kill many people as punishment for Timbuktu's defiance.

3 RISE OF THE SONGHAY EMPIRE

Sunni Ali's victory over Timbuktu was the beginning of his career as a great military leader. He went on to build the small Kingdom of Gao into the Songhay Empire. Sunni Ali won every war he fought and conquered every territory he attacked.

After conquering Timbuktu, Sunni Ali continued to fight campaigns along the Niger River. Upriver from Timbuktu, the Niger River flows through flat terrain. This causes it to spread out in a vast region of lakes and meandering waterways that form the inland delta of the Niger. The inland delta was always coveted by the surrounding peoples because of its floodplains, rich in fertile soil, and abundant

Many peoples competed for control of the inland delta of the Niger River, which is located roughly in the middle of the river's long course.

The Fulani often raided Songhay territory. A Fulani woman from the city of Mopti on the Niger River wears earrings made of pure gold, a reminder of the important role once played by the gold trade in creating the wealth of the Western Sudan.

fishing grounds in an otherwise dry land. In Sunni Ali's quest to gain more territory, he fought off the Fulani and others who wished to occupy the delta region. Many of these wars were fought on the river.

To transport his army, Sunni Ali relied on a fleet of boats manned by Sorko crewmen under a naval commander, called the *hi-koi*. This Sorko navy greatly strengthened the empire's military power by dominating the Niger River.

JENNE AND WALATA

The third most important city of the Songhay Empire was Jenne, far to the south of Timbuktu. Jenne had survived as an independent city for a long time. The entire city, as well as some of its farms and cattle herds, was encircled by a high wall. Adding to Jenne's security from invaders was the river itself. The city was surrounded by water for much of the year when the Niger River was in flood stage.

Sunni Ali took advantage of the highwater season by approaching Jenne with his fleet of some four hundred boats full of warriors. Even so, Sunni Ali could not break through the walls. His army had to maintain a siege for seven years before starvation forced the people of Jenne to surrender.

Sunni Ali also wished to conquer Walata in the Sahara Desert. Walata was the city to which the people fled when he attacked Timbuktu. Sunni Ali was so attached to his riverboats that he even wanted to use them for the campaign against that desert city. In 1480 Ali began digging a canal from Ras-el-Ma at the western end of Lake Faguibine. From there it was 120 miles (193 km) through the desert to Walata. While Sunni Ali's army was digging, he learned that other invaders were attacking Walata, so he abandoned the canal project and marched his army overland to its next battle.

DEATH OF THE SORCERER KING

Sunni Ali was a man of war. He established royal residences in four different places, including Gao and Kukiya, but he never lived in them because he was always away on military campaigns. He was the kind of ruler who could successfully sustain the empire despite the fact that its subjects frequently rebelled and hostile neighbors constantly raided its territory.

In 1492, after holding power for twenty-eight years, Sunni Ali drowned while returning from a campaign. The commanders of the Songhay army appointed his son, Baru, to succeed him as *sunni* of the empire he had created.

4 ASKIYA MUHAMMAD THE GREAT

One of Sunni Ali's army commanders was Muhammad Abu Bakr Toure. The Toure were originally a clan of the Soninke people, whose connection with Islam dated back centuries. Muhammad Toure was a devout Muslim. He had objected to Sunni Ali's brutal treatment of the Muslims when he conquered Timbuktu.

In 1493, only fourteen months after Sunni Ali's death, Muhammad Toure and the troops loyal to him defeated the army of Sunni Baru. They ended the *sunni* dynasty.

Muhammad Toure became the first *askiya*. *Askiya* was a rank in the Songhay army. When

Tomb of Askiya Muhammad the Great, in Gao, Mali

Muhammad Toure became king, he took *askiya* as his title and as the name of his new dynasty. From that time on, all the kings of Songhay were known as *askiya*.

GOVERNMENT

When Askiya Muhammad came to power, the Songhay Empire already had a well-developed system of government that had existed in the days of Sunni Ali and perhaps earlier. The territory was divided into eleven provinces, each governed by an official with the title of *koi* or *fari*. These governors were usually relatives of the *askiya*. Important towns—such as Timbuktu, Jenne, Masina, and Tagha—had governors with the title of *munjo*. Their most important duty was probably to collect taxes.

Askiya Muhammad created a powerful new post, that of *kurmina-fari*, the head of the western provinces of the empire. Among the most important other government officials were the *fari-munjo*, who were in charge of the royal lands; the *hou-kokorai-koi*, the master of the royal household; the *korei-farima*, who dealt with the neighboring Arab and Berber peoples; and the *wanei-farima*, who was responsible for the royal property acquired on military expeditions.

The chief military officers were the *hi-koi*, the master of the river fleet, and the *balama*, who was chief of the port at Kabara, Timbuktu's port. The legal system in the towns was mainly administered by *qadis*, or senior judges, who were appointed by the *askiya*. The *askiya* himself also sat in judgment of legal disputes, as did the provincial governors.

PILGRIMAGE

One of the teachings of Islam is that all Muslims who can afford it must visit Mecca, the birthplace of Muhammad the Prophet in present-day Saudi Arabia. This pilgrimage, or religious journey, is called the *hajj*.

Late in 1496, about three years after he came to power, Askiya Muhammad set off for Mecca. He was away for almost two years. This suggests that he must have been well liked by his people, despite having ended the *sunni* dynasty by forcing his way onto the throne; otherwise he would not have dared to be away so long.

The hajj added greatly to Askiya Muhammad's prestige. All who make the journey to Mecca acquire a special blessing called *baraka*. It is respected in the Western Sudan by Muslims and non-Muslims alike. Pilgrims also return with the special title *al-Hajj* (the Pilgrim). Furthermore, the Sharif of Mecca—the spiritual leader of the Islamic world—named Askiya Muhammad as his caliph, or deputy, for the Western Sudan. This greatly increased Muhammad's power at home, because it confirmed him as "Commander of the Faithful," leader of all the Muslims of the Western Sudan.

Askiya Muhammad, known as the pilgrim king, had the wholehearted support of the influential Muslim populations of the cities. The power base of Sunni Ali, the sorcerer king, had been in the rural communities where the ancestral religion was still followed.

THE EMPIRE UNDER ASKIYA MUHAMMAD

Askiya Muhammad, who came to be known as Muhammad the Great, created a professional full-time army and built up the Songhay cavalry. He expanded the Songhay boundaries far beyond the Niger waterways that had limited the campaigns of Sunni Ali and his boatmen. Under Askiya Muhammad, the Songhay Empire reached as far as Agades in the east and the upper Senegal River in the west. The empire became so large that its army was divided into two, one for the western provinces and the other for the eastern provinces.

The authors of books written in Timbuktu state that Askiya Muhammad had thirty-four sons by his various wives and concubines. Since most of these sons were half-brothers, related only through their father, they did not have the close attachment to one another that might be felt by brothers who also have the same mother.

As Askiya Muhammad's sons grew up, they began to quarrel and compete among themselves for power. When Askiya Muhammad reached about seventy years of age, he had weakened physically, and his sons began to demand that he retire in favor of one of them. He found it increasingly difficult to control his sons, and the royal court became a dangerous place for the aging man.

The leader of the angered sons was Musa, who had been appointed Askiya Muhammad's heir. The younger generation of power-hungry men were angered because Ali Fulan, who held the title *hou-kokorai-koi*, would not allow anyone to speak with the *askiya* in person. They did not know that

Under Askiya Muhammad the Great, the Songhay Empire reached as far east as Agades, in present-day Niger.

The city of Kano, in present-day Nigeria, was the center of a powerful Hausa state. Kano surrendered to the Songhay army after a long siege.

Ali Fulan was concealing the fact that Askiya Muhammad had lost his eyesight. Musa threatened to kill Ali Fulan, who fled for his life in about 1527. In the following year Musa led several of his brothers in revolt against their father. In the process, they killed one of their own uncles, who had tried to calm them down.

In August 1528, during prayers at the mosque, Musa announced that his father had been removed from office. Old, blind, and without any powerful protectors, Askiya Muhammad had no choice but to abdicate. Musa became the next *askiya* of Songhay, although his father lived another ten years.

5 RIVALRY FOR POWER

Askiya Musa had to fight his rival brothers to stay in power. He killed some of them in battle; others fled the empire. Those who remained in Gao began to disappear one after the other as Askiya Musa eliminated his rivals. Finally in 1531 some of the surviving brothers joined together and killed Musa in battle. His bloody reign had lasted only two years nine months.

The eldest of the remaining brothers was the *kurmina-fari*, or governor of the western provinces. He expected to be next in line for the kingship, so he returned to Gao. But when he and his supporting brothers arrived in the capital, they found that

Askiya Muhammad Bunkan influenced the culture of the palace, giving his courtiers colorful robes, such as those worn by these Tuareg men in the Western Sudan.

their cousin Muhammad Bunkan had seized the throne.

ASKIYA MUHAMMAD BUNKAN

Askiya Muhammad Bunkan is remembered for introducing the music of drums and trumpets into his palace and for providing the members of his court with rich costumes of imported cloth. But Muhammad Bunkan led so many campaigns and fought so many battles that the Songhay people grew tired of being at war and began to dislike him. He was also unpopular because he was cruel to the aged, blind Askiya Muhammad the Great, whom he forced out of the palace and confined to an insect-infested island in the Niger River.

Before long, Muhammad Bunkan made a mistake that would cost him his kingship. He brought back to Gao his childhood friend Ismail, one of Askiya Muhammad's many sons. Ismail had been hiding with the Tuareg to escape the fighting between his brothers. Now he returned to Gao, where Askiya Muhammad Bunkan gave him one of his daughters as a wife. This was done on the condition that Ismail swear he would never betray his old friend, who was now also his father-in-law.

Ismail was shocked to find that Muhammad Bunkan was mistreating his father, Askiya Muhammad, and humiliating his sisters by forcing them to appear at court with their faces uncovered. According to their Muslim beliefs, women who did not cover their faces were considered impure. When Ismail went to visit Askiya Muhammad on the island, the old king convinced him that Muhammad Bunkan had to be overthrown.

THE RETURN OF ASKIYA MUHAMMAD'S SONS
Ismail worked with powerful friends of his father who were still at court and deposed Muhammad Bunkan in April 1537. Muhammad Bunkan fled to Mali, and Ismail became the new *askiya*.

Askiya Ismail immediately released his father and brought him to the palace. In gratitude to his son, Askiya Muhammad presented Ismail with his caliph's costume: a green robe, green cap, white turban, and the Arabian sword that Askiya Muhammad had been given in Mecca.

Askiya Muhammad the Great lived into his nineties and died in 1538, during Ismail's reign. Like Musa, Ismail reigned for two years nine months until he died a natural death in November 1539. The leading men of Songhay peacefully agreed on electing the next *askiya*. They chose Ishaq, another son of Askiya Muhammad.

Ishaq was a poor ruler because he upset many of the Songhay people. For example, although he was a devout Muslim, Ishaq regularly sent an agent to Timbuktu to demand large sums of money from the Muslim merchants there. This hurt the economy and gained Ishaq many enemies. Ishaq became frightened and suspicious that he would be overthrown. He killed or dismissed anyone he suspected of opposing him. He appointed three separate men as *kurmina-fari* (governor of the western provinces). Ishaq executed the first one for an offense, and the second governor was caught in a conspiracy to overthrow Ishaq. The third *kurmina-fari* was Dawud, who eventually became the next *askiya*.

When Askiya Ishaq was near death, friends of Dawud called the governor to the capital to make sure he became the next *askiya*. They knew that Bokar, a handsome prince who was the son of one of Askiya Muhammad's daughters, was very popular with the people of Songhay. They feared he posed a threat to Dawud's becoming king.

Bokar did not survive this competition for power. According to legend, Dawud had him killed with a magic spell cast by a Muslim diviner.

6 DAWUD, THE LAST GREAT *ASKIYA*

Together with Sunni Ali Ber and Askiya Muhammad, Askiya Dawud is regarded as one of Songhay's three greatest rulers. His reign lasted for thirty-three years, from 1549 to 1582.

During the years of fighting between the rival brothers, Songhay's enemies had begun to raid across its borders again. Askiya Dawud moved to strengthen Songhay by leading successful military campaigns against old enemies. His only military defeat was in a raid far to the east against horsemen of the Hausa city-state of Katsina.

Askiya Dawud had received a solid Islamic education. He is said to have memorized the

Children in Timbuktu are taught in Arabic and sometimes use washable ink on wooden boards to write their lessons. Today, Timbuktu remains a center of scholarship.

entire Muslim holy book, the *Koran*. Even when he was *askiya,* Dawud continued his studies of Islamic scripture and law. He was generous to Islamic scholars, giving them gifts of land, cattle, slaves, grain, and clothing. Timbuktu reached the peak of its prosperity during the reign of Askiya Dawud, and he contributed generously to restoration of the main mosque there. When he passed that way on military campaigns he always stopped in Timbuktu.

Relations between Songhay kings and the Timbuktu scholars had changed significantly since the days of Sunni Ali. The leading men of Timbuktu continued to believe that their authority was independent of the Songhay kings, the belief for which Sunni Ali had punished them when he had conquered the city. But Askiya Dawud, an educated Muslim himself, did not challenge the scholars' authority.

One famous event shows just how different Dawud's approach was from Sunni Ali's. Hurtful gossip had once led to a misunderstanding between Dawud and the *qadi*, or senior judge, of Timbuktu. On an expedition to Mali, Askiya Dawud stopped in Timbuktu, but the *qadi* refused to see him. If this had happened to Sunni Ali, the *qadi* would probably have been killed. But Askiya Dawud allowed himself to be kept waiting for a long time outside the *qadi*'s home. When he was finally allowed to enter, he humbled himself before the Muslim leader until their relationship was repaired.

Up to the reign of Askiya Dawud, all of the

askiya rulers of Songhay had been Askiya Muhammad's sons, with the exception of the *usurper* Muhammad Bunkan. Many other sons of Askiya Muhammad had held high offices and titles in the empire. As these offices became vacant during the thirty-three years of Askiya Dawud's reign, he appointed his own sons to fill them. In this way Dawud gradually eliminated from high office the descendants of his brothers, who were also sons of Askiya Muhammad. From then on, all the rulers of Songhay were descendants of Askiya Dawud. After Askiya Dawud died in 1582, however, warfare broke out once again as his sons fought for power.

FEUDING BROTHERS

The next *askiya* was one of Dawud's sons, Askiya al-Hajj. Troubles between him and some of his brothers caused al-Hajj to be deposed in 1586. He was replaced by Muhammad Bani, another of Dawud's sons. Some people regarded Muhammad Bani as the most foolish of all the brothers. They tried to depose him, but their plot was discovered, and they were severely punished.

CIVIL WAR

At the beginning of Muhammad Bani's reign, the town of Kabara was the scene of events that led to a civil war, which ultimately proved disastrous for the Songhay Empire. Kabara is Timbuktu's port, a few miles away on the Niger River.

At that time, two of the most powerful men in Songhay lived in Kabara. One of them was Chief Alu, the *balama,* or chief of the port, who was loyal to Askiya Muhammad Bani. The other was Muhammad Sadiq, the *kurmina-fari,* who was head of the western provinces and commanded the army of western Songhay. Muhammad Sadiq was also a son of Askiya Dawud and had good relations with the leading men of Timbuktu.

In 1588 Chief Alu beat and jailed one of Commander Muhammad Sadiq's men. In response, Sadiq killed Chief Alu. Since Alu was associated with Askiya Muhammad Bani, Commander Sadiq feared that the *askiya,* his brother, would seek revenge. Sadiq and another brother, who was also an army commander, decided that their best hope was to combine their two armies, march against Gao, and depose Askiya Muhammad Bani. This eventually led to a civil war, with the western Songhay army, based at Timbuktu, fighting the army of eastern Songhay, based at Gao. Askiya Muhammad Bani died on the very day the Songhay army set out from Gao to meet the western army led by Commander Sadiq.

After a bloody battle in which a great many troops were killed on both sides, the army of Gao defeated the troops from Timbuktu. Commander Muhammad Sadiq was hunted down and killed. All of the other army commanders of the western provinces, many of whom were princes of the royal family, were imprisoned.

The new *askiya,* Ishaq II, appointed new commanders, but he could not replace the troops that had been killed. Most of the soldiers who had supported Commander Sadiq never returned from battle. Songhay lost nearly half of its army as a result of this civil war. This weakened the empire to such an extent that it was vulnerable to attack from outside forces.

THE FALL OF THE EMPIRE

For many centuries Songhay had been involved in trans-Saharan trade with Morocco. Moroccan traders lived in Songhay, and Songhay merchants stayed in Moroccan cities. The kings of Morocco were well informed about Songhay and were attracted by stories of its wealth. For the weakened Songhay Empire this was a dangerous situation, because Morocco was at the peak of its power.

THE SULTANATE OF MOROCCO

Ten years before the Songhay civil war, in 1578, Morocco had been invaded by the Portuguese with an army of twenty-five thousand soldiers. The

Moroccans had won a great victory over the Portuguese at the battle of Al-Ksar al-Kabir. Only a few hundred Portuguese soldiers survived to tell the tale; many became prisoners. This has been called one of the most decisive battles of world history, because for many years it discouraged Europeans from further efforts to conquer North Africa. It also shows how strong Morocco was at that time. The Sultan of Morocco, however, had been killed in his hour of victory. He was immediately succeeded by his twenty-nine-year-old brother, Mulay Ahmad, who received the title al-Mansur, meaning the victorious.

Sultan Mulay al-Mansur was a skillful ruler. He strengthened his kingdom through diplomacy and military campaigns that ended internal conflicts. His diplomats ensured good relations with foreign powers by giving rich gifts to other rulers. But this drained the Moroccan royal treasury.

Mulay al-Mansur decided to rebuild the Moroccan treasury by capturing Songhay's wealth. In 1583, five years before the Songhay civil war, he hired an Arab merchant named Ibn al-Filali, who lived in Gao, to act as a spy in Songhay.

THE SULTAN'S CONQUEST

After the civil war broke out in Songhay, Ibn al-Filali informed Sultan Mulay al-Mansur that it had greatly weakened the Songhay Empire. In 1589 the Moroccans forged a letter that they claimed had been sent to the sultan by a brother of Askiya Ishaq II. The man they claimed was the *askiya*'s brother was really a slave who had escaped from the Songhay royal household and fled to Morocco. In the forged letter, the *askiya*'s "brother" asked Mulay al-Mansur to aid Songhay rebels in overthrowing the *askiya*.

The letter was sent to Askiya Ishaq II early in 1590, with a demand to surrender and accept Moroccan authority. Askiya Ishaq II failed to take this threat seriously. He was so unconcerned about the Moroccans that, instead of preparing for an invasion from the north, he took his troops on an expedition far to the west of the empire. Askiya Ishaq II was still far from home with his troops when he received news that the Moroccan army was on its way.

The Moroccan army had set out at the end of 1590 with 4,600 experienced fighters. They were

A Tuareg camp. Askiya Ishaq's order to fill in the desert water holes was never carried out because Tuareg raiders attacked the Songhay messengers who carried the order.

led by Judar Pasha, a Spanish Christian who had converted to Islam. His army included many Portuguese and Spanish prisoners who had been captured by the Moroccans at the battle of Al-Ksar al-Kabir twelve years earlier. Faced with imprisonment, slavery, or death, they chose to convert to Islam and serve in the Moroccan army. Among them were five hundred horsemen armed with guns, called *arquebuses*, which were the most up-to-date weapon of the day. An additional 1,500 horsemen carried long spears, and they took along ten cannons that fired stone cannonballs.

When the Songhay received warning of the Moroccan invasion, Muhammad Gao, who was then commander of the western troops, wanted to go out and fill in the desert wells so that the invaders could not find water. This was a good plan, but the *askiya* ignored his advice. Instead, Askiya Ishaq II sent messengers to tribal chiefs asking them to fill in the desert water holes. The messengers never got through because they were attacked by Tuareg raiders.

If the Songhay had attacked while the Moroccans were exhausted from the two-month journey across the desert, they might have been victorious. But Askiya Ishaq's troops had been quickly assembled and were disorganized. The Moroccans had a week to recover before the war began.

SONGHAY DEFEATED
The decisive battle took place on March 12, 1591, at Tondibi on the east bank of the Niger River

about 35 miles (56 km) north of Gao. The Song-hay army contained as many as forty thousand men, but it could not compete with the superior firepower of Judar's disciplined troops. The Song-hay suffered heavy losses. As they retreated across the Niger River, courageous Songhay soldiers tied themselves together and continued to shoot arrows at the advancing Moroccans until the Songhay troops died in hand-to-hand combat.

Askiya Ishaq II offered the Moroccans a tribute of 100,000 pieces of gold and one thousand slaves, hoping this would satisfy them and that they would leave Songhay. By that time the Moroccan troops were exhausted and ill. Judar Pasha was prepared to accept the tribute and retreat back across the desert.

Sultan Mulay al-Mansur, however, wanted his army to occupy the newly conquered land below the desert. He angrily rejected Askiya Ishaq's offer and replaced Judar Pasha with another general, also named Mansur, who was instructed to complete the conquest of Songhay. The Moroccans occupied Timbuktu, Gao, and Jenne. They looted these cities on the Niger and sent the wealth back to Marrakesh, where it was used to fill the treasury and build fine palaces.

When the Songhay cavalry retreated into the countryside, they deposed Askiya Ishaq II. In his place they named Commander Muhammad Gao as the new *askiya.*

Muhammad Gao had shown wisdom as the commander who had wanted to fill in the desert water holes. Later, as *askiya,* he unwisely accepted an invitation to visit Mansur, the new Moroccan general, and was assassinated.

END OF THE EMPIRE

The Songhay army had been defeated in battle and driven from their trading cities. However, Songhay soldiers continued to resist the Moroccans with surprise attacks throughout the countryside. Succeeding *askiyas* continually sent raiding parties to attack Moroccan guard posts and troops. But the Songhay government had been weakened beyond recovery. The *askiya's* former subjects revolted, and the *askiyas* were never able to recover their empire. The Songhay Empire had fallen to the Moroccans.

A weaver in Niamey, in modern-day Niger, makes cloth. Niamey is in the Dendi region, where many Songhay continued to live under their own *askiyas* after the Songhay Empire had been conquered by Morocco.

Far to the south, however, many Songhay people continued to live independently in their ancient homeland of Dendi. Under their own *askiyas*, they were hardly touched by Moroccan rule.

8 A LASTING LEGACY

Together the Songhay Empire and its predecessor, the Kingdom of Gao, formed a powerful West African state that lasted some nine hundred years, making it one of the longest to endure anywhere in the world.

Many times in world history vast regions have been conquered by strong leaders who then found it impossible to maintain rule over the lands they had conquered. Their empires soon disappeared. The Songhay state survived for so long because it successfully brought together peoples of many cultures. These peoples developed a thriving trade network and a complex system of government that

The Songhay Empire successfully united peoples of many ethnic backgrounds, which was one of its great strengths. A Bozo elder from Timbuktu wears an embroidered *boubou*, or gown.

made success possible for many centuries.

Even today the Songhay in the countryside of Mali and Niger recall their great god-like hero. They call him simply "The Shi." Others know him as Sunni Ali, the leader who founded one of Africa's greatest empires.

TIMELINE

A. D. c. 679	The dynasty of rulers carrying the title of *za* is founded at Kukiya
c. 750	Gao becomes an important trading city
c. 1010	Za Kossoi becomes a Muslim
c. 1100	Timbuktu is founded
c. 1300	The *za* dynasty of rulers is replaced by those carrying the title of *sunni*
c. 1310-30	Songhay begins to be ruled by Mali
c. 1375-1400	Songhay regains its independence from Mali
1464	Sunni Ali comes to power and begins to conquer neighboring peoples
1468-69	Sunni Ali captures Timbuktu
1470-76	Sunni Ali captures Jenne
1492	Sunni Ali drowns while returning from a military campaign
1493	Muhammad Toure ends the *sunni* dynasty and becomes the first *askiya*
1496-98	Askiya Muhammad makes the pilgrimage to Mecca
1528	Askiya Muhammad is removed from office and replaced by one of his sons
1549-1582	Askiya Dawud reigns
1591	Songhay is invaded by the Moroccan army and defeated at the Battle of Tondibi

RULING DYNASTIES

OF THE KINGDOM OF GAO AND THE SONGHAY EMPIRE

The earliest rulers of Gao went by the title of *za*. According to tradition, there were fifteen *za* up to the time of Za Kossoi, who converted to Islam in the year 1010. The *za* dynasty continued for more than three hundred years until it ended in 1335 with the first of the kings known as *sunni*. During the time of the *sunni*, the Kingdom of Gao expanded to become the Songhay Empire. The *sunni* ruled until 1493, when Muhammad Toure founded the *askiya* dynasty.

The three greatest kings of Songhay each led the empire through important periods of expansion. The first was from 1464 to 1492 under Sunni

Ali. The second was from 1493 to 1528 under Askiya Muhammad the Great. The third was from 1549 to 1582 under Askiya Dawud. Historians believe there were twelve *askiyas* altogether, including Muhammad Gao and two others who carried the title after the Moroccan invasion:

Muhammad the Great	1493-1528
Musa	1528-31
Muhammad Bunkan	1531-37
Ismail	1537-39
Ishaq I	1539-49
Dawud	1549-82
al-Hajj	1582-86
Muhammad Bani	1586-88
Ishaq II	1588-91
Muhammad Gao	1591-92?

After Askiya Muhammad Gao was lured to his death by the Moroccan general, two other sons of Askiya Dawud held the title of askiya at the same time. One of them lived at Timbuktu as a puppet ruler of the Moroccan government. The other was at Dendi, from where he continued to lead Songhay resistance against the Moroccan occupation.

GLOSSARY

al-Hajj the Pilgrim; honorary title given to one who has made the hajj

Arabic language of Arabia; believed by Muslims to be the language in which Allah revealed the Koran to the Prophet Muhammad

archaeologist scientist who recovers, studies, and interprets evidence about how people lived long ago

arquebus early type of firearm that used a primitive method of igniting gunpowder

askiya title of king of Songhay of *askiya* dynasty; originally a rank in the Songhay army

balama chief of port at Kabara, the port of Timbuktu

baraka blessing received by pilgrims who make the hajj

diviner priest or priestess with special means of foretelling future events

fari government official; governor of a Songhay province

fari-munjo official in charge of the royal lands

hajj pilgrimage to Mecca and Medina undertaken by many Muslims in accordance with Muslim teaching

hi-koi commander of the Songhay river fleet

hou-kokorai-koi official in charge of the royal household

Islam religion that holds that Allah is the one God

koi government official; governor of a Songhay province

Koran holy book of Islam that Muslims believe was revealed to Muhammad by Allah

korei-farima official responsible for relations with Arab and Berber traders and settlers

kurmina-fari governor of the western provinces and commander of its army, always of the royal family, second only to the *askiya* in power

mosque Muslim house of worship

munjo governor of a major city

Muslim member of the Islamic faith

qadi senior judge in Islamic society

sorcerer person with magical powers

siege military blockade of a protected place to force it to surrender

usurper one who seizes power by force and without right

wanei-farima official responsible for the booty captured on military expeditions

za king, in the Tuareg language

FOR FURTHER READING

Adeleke, Tunde. *Songhay*. New York: The Rosen Publishing Group, 1996.

Johnson, John W., Thomas A. Hale, and Stephen Belcher. *Oral Epics from Africa: Vibrant Voices from a Vast Continent.* Bloomington and Indianapolis: Indiana University Press, 1997.

Mann, Kenny. *Ghana, Mali, Songhay: The Western Sudan.* Parsippany, NJ: Dillon Press, 1996.

FOR ADVANCED READERS

McKissick, Patricia, and Frederick McKissick. *The Royal Kingdoms of Ghana, Mali and Songhay: Life in Medieval Africa.* New York: Henry Holt & Co., 1994.

WEB SITES

Due to the changeable nature of the Internet, sites appear and disappear very quickly. Internet addresses must be entered with capital and lowercase letters exactly as they appear.

Africa information page: http://www.H-AFRICA@h-net. msu.edu

Connections page: http://www.asu.alasu.edu/academic/advstudies/1d.html

The Baobab Project: http://www.web-dubois-fas.harvard.edu/Dubois/Baobab/baobab.html

INDEX

ABOUT THE AUTHOR

David Conrad is an associate professor of history at the State University of New York–Oswego. He holds a Ph.D. in African History from the School of Oriental and African Studies at the University of London. His research focuses on early kingdoms of the Western Sudan, the influence of Islam on sub-Saharan cultures, and the Mande-speaking peoples. He is editor and co-translator of *A State of Intrigue: The Epic of Bamana Segu,* and editor (with Barbara Frank) of *Status and Identity in West Africa: Nyamakalaw of Mande.* He has published many professional articles.